D1312480

PuzzleMania®
Animal Friends

HIGHLIGHTS PRESS

Honesdale, Pennsylvania

CONTENTS

When you finish a puzzle, check it off √.
Good luck, and happy puzzling!

Gone Fishing

Brooke and three friends went fish shopping at the pet store. From the clues below, can you figure out what color fish each friend got and what tank decoration each picked out?

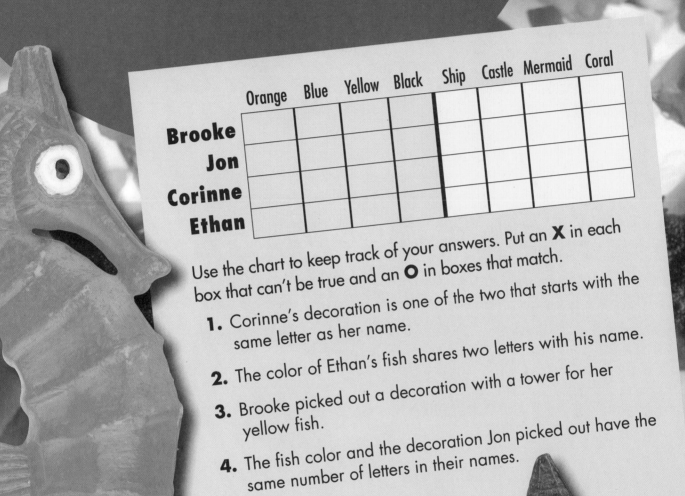

	Orange	Blue	Yellow	Black	Ship	Castle	Mermaid	Coral
Brooke								
Jon								
Corinne								
Ethan								

Use the chart to keep track of your answers. Put an **X** in each box that can't be true and an **O** in boxes that match.

1. Corinne's decoration is one of the two that starts with the same letter as her name.

2. The color of Ethan's fish shares two letters with his name.

3. Brooke picked out a decoration with a tower for her yellow fish.

4. The fish color and the decoration Jon picked out have the same number of letters in their names.

Peanut Gallery

These elephants are cooling off. While they do, Take a good look at the scene. There are **25** peanuts hidden here. Can you find them all?

Illustrated by Kevin Rechin

Check...and Double Check

There are at least **19** differences between these pictures. How many can you find?

Double Cross

To find the "purr-fect" answer to the riddle below, first cross out all the pairs of matching letters. Then write the remaining letters in order in the spaces beneath the riddle.

AA	TT	II	TH	SS	QQ	EY
HH	OO	BB	RR	AL	EE	VV
LH	NN	ZZ	YY	CC	AV	AA
II	QQ	EE	EN	DD	PP	WW
IN	GG	LL	TT	VV	EL	ZZ
XX	HH	IV	II	BB	OO	SS
TT	UU	NN	EE	SS	ES	MM

Why are cats good at video games?

☐ ☐ ☐ ☐   ☐ ☐ ☐   ☐ ☐ ☐ ☐

☐ ☐ ☐ ☐   ☐ ☐ ☐ ☐ ☐ .

Animal Addition

Each animal in the equations on this page has a value from 1 to 9. No two animals have the same value. Can you figure out which numbers go with which animals? Here's a hint to help you get started: The frog has the highest number; the rabbit has the lowest number.

Illustrated by David Helton

Hidden Pictures®
Crazy for Coconuts

 snake

 seashell

 ice-cream cone

 elf's hat

 chili pepper

candle

 fish

crown

 spoon

lightning bolt

 pennant

 slice of pie

 puzzle piece

 bowl

 muffin

 heart

starfish

 crescent moon

 knitted hat

 9

Feathered Nests

Choosing the right birdhouse is a big decision for these birds, but your only job is to find the hidden objects.

boomerang

ladle

high-heeled shoe

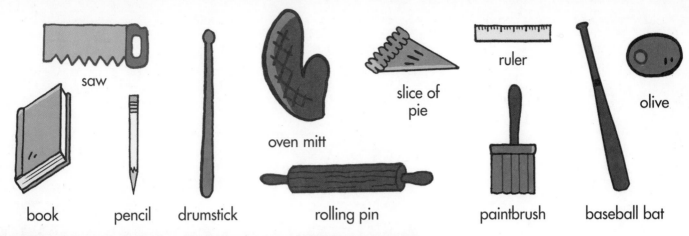

saw

book · pencil · drumstick

oven mitt

rolling pin

slice of pie

ruler

olive

paintbrush · baseball bat

SOLD!

OPEN

FOR SALE

OPEN HOUSE

For the Birds

Can you tell which bird name is real and which one is made up in each pair below? We circled the first real one.

Scarlet tanager
Blue tangerine

Orange-nosed songbird
Red-winged blackbird

Smidgeon
Pigeon

Common loon
Buffoon

Great blue heron
Good green goober

Waltzing matilda
Whippoorwill

Little egret
No regrets

Kookybird
Cockatiel

Illustrated by Neil Numberman

11

Double Coasters

There are at least 20 differences between these two pictures. How many can you find?

Find the turtle that is different.

Hidden Pictures®
Polar Bear Club

top hat

banana

heart

boot

bird

ice-cream cone

bat

slice of pie

hammer

mitten

toothbrush

snake

paper clip

sailboat

14

Check...and Double Check

There are at least **18** differences between these pictures. How many can you find?

Pet Q's

Woof or Meow?

Some of these are dog breeds and some are cat breeds. Can you figure out which is which?

BEAGLE
COLLIE
DALMATIAN
MANX
PERSIAN
POINTER
PUG
RAGDOLL
SIAMESE
WHIPPET

Arf.

Missing Vowels

RDNT is the word *rodent* with the vowels taken away. Can you figure out the name of these five pet rdnts?

_____

RT

_____

MS

_____

HMSTR

_____

GRBL

_____

GN PG

Guess Who?

Can you tell what these two pets are?

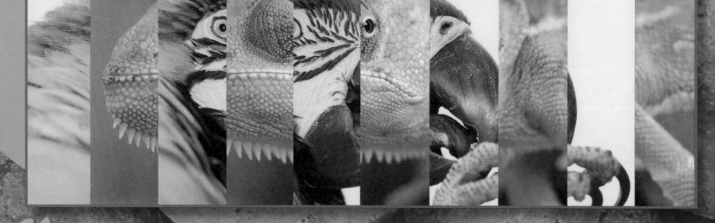

A Pet What???

Which pet is Archie walking?

JUMBLed PetS

Unscramble each set of letters to get the name of a pet.

SHIF — — — —

RUTTLE — — — — — —

TERFER — — — — — —

RYNACA — — — — — —

BITBAR — — — — — —

Which two goldfish are exactly alike?

Leaping Lemurs

The lemurs that live in these trees have a rule. When they are finished, every row of trees across, down, and diagonally will have **30** lemurs. We've written the correct number on some trees. Use this information to figure out how many lemurs belong on the others. Write the correct number on each tree.

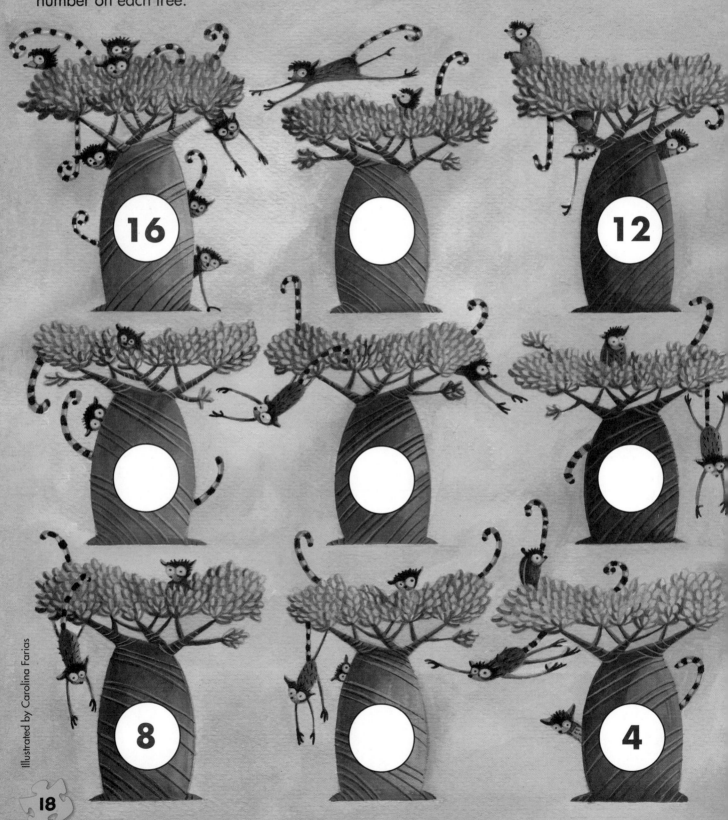

Space Scramble

These astro-animals are ready to return home. Unscramble the letters on each shuttle to see which animal belongs inside. Then find the hidden words in the grid below to locate each one's home continent. Answers in the grid can be found up and down and across. We have located the first continent for you.

A	N	A	R	A	N	O	R	E	P	A	A	F
U	P	N	S	U	S	T	T	U	M	F	S	I
S	T	T	A	R	T	W	H	Q	A	R	I	A
R	R	A	L	C	R	A	A	M	E	R	C	A
U	I	W	I	T	I	L	I	R	M	I	W	H
Z	S	A	O	C	A	A	A	D	C	A	F	

nadap

meu

rifegaf

granooka

neunpig

ladb aglee

Puzzle by Radha HS

Illustrated by Dave Clegg

MONKEY BUSINESS

It's time to monkey around! Each of these primate names fits into the grid in just one way. Use the size of each word as a clue to where it might fit. When you're done, write the letters from the shaded squares in order in the spaces below to see the answer to the riddle.

Word List

3 letters
APE

4 letters
~~DOUC~~

5 letters
LEMUR
LORIS
POTTO

6 letters
AYE-AYE
BABOON
BONOBO
GALAGO
GIBBON
LANGUR
MONKEY

7 letters
COLOBUS
GORILLA
MACAQUE
TAMARIN
TARSIER

8 letters
MANDRILL
MARMOSET

9 letters
ORANGUTAN

10 letters
CHIMPANZEE

D O U C

When do monkeys play baseball?

Tic Tac Row

Each of these horses has something in common with the other two horses in the same row. For example, in the first row across, all three horses have spots. Look at the other rows across, down, and diagonally. Can you tell what's alike in each row?

Penguin Path

This penguin is hungry! Can you help him slip and slide down a path that leads into the water so he can fish for food? Be careful not to crash into any other penguins.

Start

Finish

23

Hidden Pictures®
Boarding Buddies

fork

handbell

glove

mitten

crescent moon

saw

These animals are making a splash! Can you find all the hidden objects?

pencil

sock

tack

ladle

banana

leaf

Illustrated by Iryna Bodnaruk

25

It's Fishy!

If you like to go fishing, you've come to the right puzzle.
Each fish in this aquarium has one that looks exactly like it.
Can you fish out all the matching pairs?

Moo-ve It Along

These five cows have wandered away from their owners. Using the clues below, can you figure out which cow belongs to which rancher?

Moosic

Munch

Cowly

Cuddles

Ferdie

Use the chart to keep track of your answers. Put an **X** in each box that can't be true and an **O** in boxes that match.

	Moosic	Munch	Cowly	Cuddles	Ferdie
Buck					
Jeannie					
Roy					
Sasha					
Tex					

1. Buck's cow is two colors.

2. Jeannie and her cow have the same number of letters in their names.

3. Tex is not fond of longhorns, but he likes bells.

4. Sasha's cow, which does not have horns, is the same color as another cow, but not the same color as Buck's cow.

Illustrated by Dave Clegg   Puzzle by Lori Mortensen

Hamming It Up

Use the clues below to fill in the answer spaces. Each answer includes the letters **H-A-M.** If you can solve them all, you are a true c**HAM**pion!

1. Tool used for pounding nails   H A M **M E R**

2. Small, furry pet   H A M __ __ __ __

3. A type of shark   H A M __ __ __ __ __ __

4. What you wash your hair with   __ H A M __ __ __

5. Container for dirty clothes   H A M __ __ __

6. A bed that hangs between two trees   H A M __ __ __ __

7. A symbol of St. Patrick's Day   __ H A M __ __ __ __

8. A sweet cracker   __ __ __ H A M

9. President Lincoln's first name   __ __ __ __ __ H A M

10. A leg muscle   H A M __ __ __ __ __ __

11. A popular food at cookouts   H A M __ __ __ __ __ __

12. A New England state   __ __ __ __ H A M __ __ __ __ __

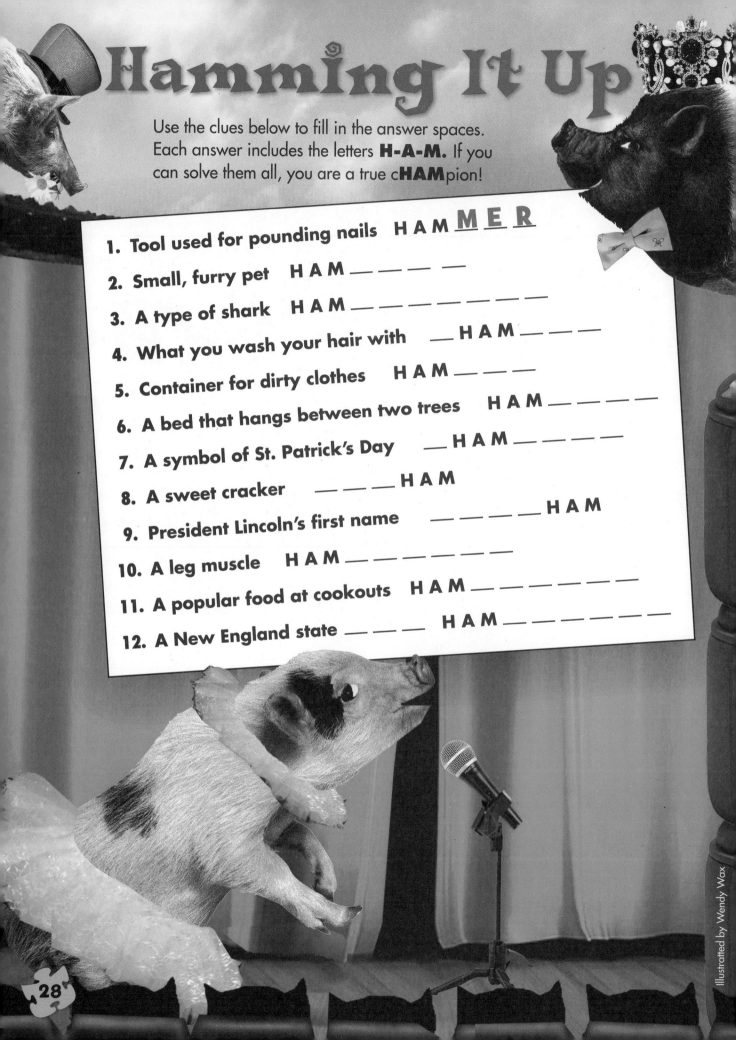

Illustrated by Wendy Wax

Hidden Pictures® Checkmate!

crescent moon

eyeglasses

comb

elf's hat

pencil

sailboat

ice-cream cone

artist's brush

ruler

paper clip

doughnut

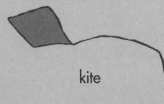
kite

drinking straw

mitten

slice of pizza

29

Illustrated by Nuno Alexandre Vieira

Box Out!

Follow the directions to cross out certain boxes. When you're done, write the remaining letters in order from left to right and top to bottom. They will give you the answer to the riddle.

Cross out all numbers divisible by 4.

Cross out all numbers divisible by 5.

M ~~8~~	A 11	Y 40	N 24	N 17	A 12
O 19	M 16	C 23	E 20	C 15	A 30
L 32	I 25	F 4	T 31	O 10	O 34
R 45	P 18	D 5	R 55	X 28	Y 44
Z 35	E 20	U 38	B 65	T 25	W 52
S 22	K 36	N 48	H 50	N 60	S 26

What do you call a cat that has lost one of its nine lives?

__ __   __ __ __ __ __ - __ __ __ __ __

Illustrated by Brian White

Hidden Pictures®
Fiesta Del Mar

snake

cane

fork

hammer

puzzle piece

boomerang

book

horseshoe

mushroom

slice of watermelon

measuring cup

sailboat

sock

banana

candy corn

tack

crown

pencil

piece of candy

bird

bell

31

Maximilian, a howler monkey, is running late to meet his friends for **Lunch at The Banana Café.** But a number of obstacles stand in his way. Use your finger to trace a path that will lead Max to his friends and to a delicious banana banquet.

START

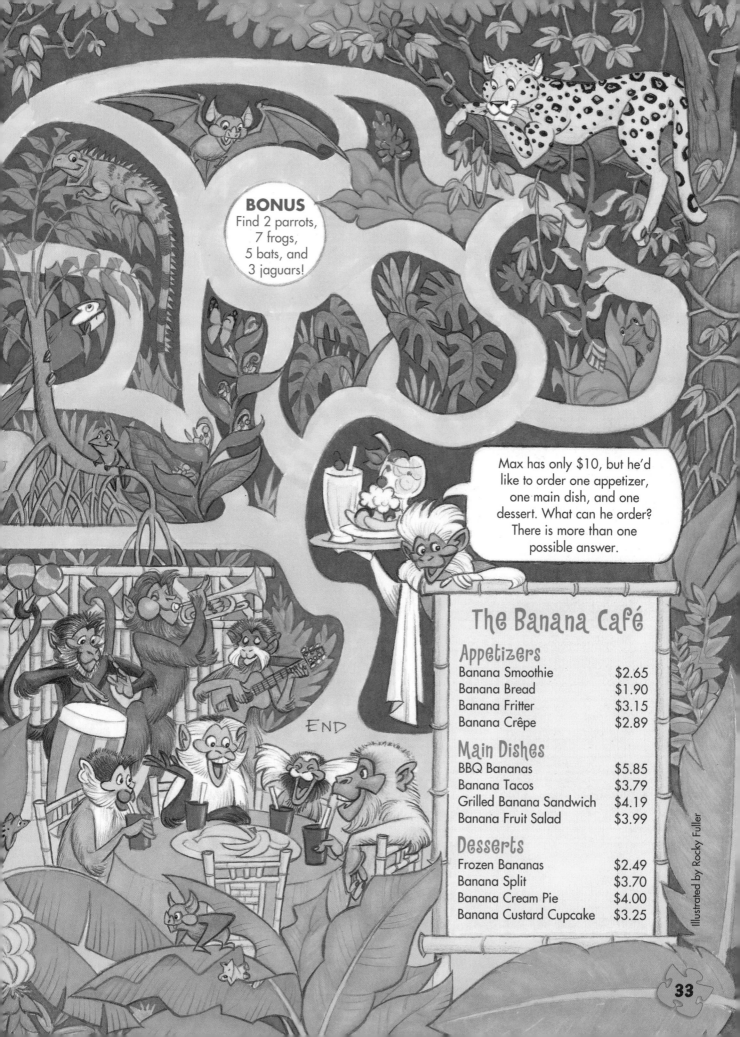

BONUS
Find 2 parrots,
7 frogs,
5 bats, and
3 jaguars!

Max has only $10, but he'd like to order one appetizer, one main dish, and one dessert. What can he order? There is more than one possible answer.

The Banana Café

Appetizers
Banana Smoothie	$2.65
Banana Bread	$1.90
Banana Fritter	$3.15
Banana Crêpe	$2.89

Main Dishes
BBQ Bananas	$5.85
Banana Tacos	$3.79
Grilled Banana Sandwich	$4.19
Banana Fruit Salad	$3.99

Desserts
Frozen Bananas	$2.49
Banana Split	$3.70
Banana Cream Pie	$4.00
Banana Custard Cupcake	$3.25

END

Illustrated by Rocky Fuller

Check...and Double Check

There are at least **17** differences between these pictures. How many can you find?

Tic Tac Row

Each of these cats has something in common with the other two cats in the same row. For example, in the top row across, each cat has a striped tail. Look at the other rows across, down, and diagonally. Can you tell what's alike in each row?

Illustrated by Carolina Farias

Horse Q's

Horse or Not?

Each pair of words has one horse and one faker. Circle the horses.

Appaloosa or Apple crisp?

Hay bale or Clydesdale?

Palomino or Domino?

Muzzle or Mustang?

Arabian or Caribbean?

Morning or Morgan?

Changing Horses

These pictures may look alike, but take a closer peek. Can you spot five differences between the two pictures?

ON Horseback

"Equestrian" is a word for a horseback rider. Can you make at least **15** words from the letters in **EQUESTRIAN**?

_____   _____   _____

_____   _____   _____

_____   _____   _____

_____   _____   _____

_____   _____   _____

Going Buggy

Which horse is leading this cart?

Horse Talk

Here are six horse sayings and their definitions. Can you guess which are true (**T**) and which are false (**F**)?

1. If someone tells you to **hold your horses**, they want you to wait. **T   F**

2. A **dark horse** is someone who is very fashionable. **T   F**

3. If information comes **straight from the horse's mouth**, it's probably false. **T   F**

4. To **horse around** is to have fun with friends. **T   F**

5. Someone who has **horse sense** uses good judgment. **T   F**

6. A **one-horse town** is a large, lively city. **T   F**

Horse Hee-Haw

Fill in the speech bubble!

Puzzles by Carly Schuna

Illustrated by Mike Moran

Zoo Hullabaloo

What a wild scene! There are some strange sights at the zoo today. Can you find at least **25** odd, weird, or wacky things in this picture?

Illustrated by Peter Grosshauser

Hidden Pictures®
Barnyard Games

feather

butter knife

strawberry

paper clip

ladle

sock

hockey stick

needle

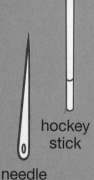
mitten

40

ruler

coat hanger

paintbrush

crescent moon

fishhook

flag

envelope

heart

mushroom

light bulb

Zoo Crew

Can you find **23** different zoo animals hiding in this puzzle? They are hidden up, down, across, backwards, and diagonally.

Word List

~~APE~~	ELEPHANT	OSTRICH
BAT	FISH	OWL
BEAR	FOX	PEACOCK
BIRD	HIPPOPOTAMUS	SNAKE
CAMEL	JAGUAR	TAPIR
CHEETAH	LION	TIGER
DEER	MONKEY	TURTLE
EAGLE	ORANGUTAN	

```
            R H                    B L E
      A C S L              B     A W X
    U A H I E M            A     T O
    G M A O F T L          T     F Z
  A E T N T N R E G I      T     X
J L E O R A N G U T A N    N     P
B E   A R H M O N K E Y    E     R
H I   P P O P O T A M U S  A
C V H E E K A N S O I E Y
K U L A R I P A T S E L
N E O C            T     R I C H
E B P O C            R U T O
L I D C              H   T
C R O K
A D E E R
```

Illustrated by Evan Polenghi

Piggy Problem

The barnyard is big, and this little piggy is lost. Help him find a path to his family so he can take a nice, cool mud bath.

SEED

43

Hidden Pictures®
Elephant Family

sailboat

fish

comb

candle

ice-cream cone

needle

paper clip

banana

open book

toothbrush

bell

heart

3 Gone Fishing

Brooke: yellow, castle   Jon: blue, ship
Corinne: black, coral
Ethan: orange, mermaid

4–5 Peanut Gallery

6 Check . . . and Double Check

7 Double Cross

AA	TT	II	(TH)	SS	QQ	(EY)
HH	OO	BB	RR	(AL)	EE	VV
(LH)	NN	ZZ	YY	CC	(AV)	AA
II	QQ	EE	(EN)	DD	PP	WW
(IN)	GG	LL	TT	VV	(EL)	ZZ
XX	HH	(IV)	II	BB	OO	SS
TT	UU	NN	EE	SS	(ES)	MM

Why are cats good at video games?
THEY ALL HAVE NINE LIVES.

8 Animal Addition

=1
=6
=2
=7
=3
=8
=4
=9
=5

9 Crazy for Coconuts

10–11 Feathered Nests

Scarlet Tanager
Red-winged Blackbird
Pigeon
Common Loon

Great Blue Heron
Whippoorwill
Little Egret
Cockatiel

12–13 Double Coasters

45

Answers

14 Polar Bear Club

15 Check . . . and Double Check

16–17 Pet Q's

Woof or Meow

BEAGLE	DOG
COLLIE	DOG
DALMATIAN	DOG
MANX	CAT
PERSIAN	CAT
POINTER	DOG
PUG	DOG
RAGDOLL	CAT
SIAMESE	CAT
WHIPPET	DOG

Missing Vowels

RT	RAT
MS	MOUSE
HMSTR	HAMSTER
GRBL	GERBIL
GN PG	GUINEA PIG

Guess Who?

It is a parrot and a chameleon.

Twin Swimmers

A Pet What???

Jumbled Pets

SHIF	RUTTLE	TERFER	RYNACA	BITBAR
FISH	TURTLE	FERRET	CANARY	RABBIT

18 Leaping Lemurs

19 Space Scramble

A	N	A	R	A	N	O	R	E	P	A	A	F
U	P	N	S	U	S	T	T	U	M	F	S	I
S	T	T	A	R	T	W	H	Q	A	R	I	A
R	R	A	L	C	R	A	A	M	E	R	C	A
U	I	W	I	T	I	L	I	R	M	I	W	H
E	Z	S	A	O	C	A	A	A	D	C	A	F

Emu (Australia)

Penguin (Antarctica)

Kangaroo (Australia)

Bald Eagle (North America)

Giraffe (Africa)

Panda (Asia)

20–21 Monkey Business

When do monkeys play baseball?
IN APE-RIL

22 Tic Tac Row

teeth brown bridle braided tail

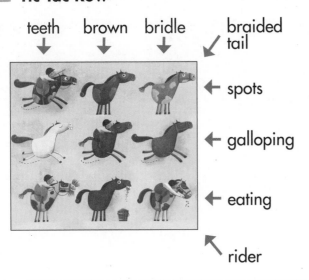

← spots

← galloping

← eating

rider

23 Penguin Path

24-25 Boarding Buddies

26 It's Fishy!

27 Moo-ve It Along

Buck: Cowly   Sasha: Ferdie
Jeannie: Cuddles   Tex: Moosic
Roy: Munch

29 Checkmate!

28 Hamming It Up

1. HAMMER
2. HAMSTER
3. HAMMERHEAD
4. SHAMPOO
5. HAMPER
6. HAMMOCK
7. SHAMROCK
8. GRAHAM
9. ABRAHAM
10. HAMSTRING
11. HAMBURGER
12. NEW HAMPSHIRE

47

Answers

30 Box Out!

What do you call a cat that has lost one of its nine lives?

AN OCTO-PUSS

31 Fiesta Del Mar

32–33 Lunch at The Banana Café

ONE POSSIBLE ANSWER:
Banana Bread $1.90 + Banana Tacos $3.79 + Frozen Bananas $2.49 = $8.18

34 Check . . . and Double Check

35 Tic Tac Row

ball of yarn   sleeping   bowl   tail up

striped tail →

bed →

black →

collar ↗

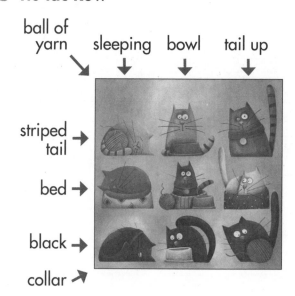

36–37 Horse Q's

Going Buggy

Horse or Not?

The real horses are
Appaloosa
Clydesdale
Palomino
Mustang
Arabian
Morgan

Changing Horses

On Horseback

Here are some words we found. You may have found others.

ant	rise	tan
nest	run	tea
net	rut	tease
nut	see	tee
quaint	set	ten
quest	sit	tin
rant	site	tine
rest	stain	train

Horse Talk

1. True
2. False
3. False
4. True
5. True
6. False

48